The Commuter's Tale

Oliver Gozzard

DESERT ♥ HEARTS

Other titles from Desert Hearts:

The Little Big Woman Book by *Llewella Gideon*

And on Piano... Nicky Hopkins by *Julian Dawson*

The Vibrators: 21 Years of Punk Mania by *Ian 'Knox' Carnochan*

Andrew Lloyd Webber: The Musical by *Nick Awde*

Sherman's Wife: A Wartime Childhood amongst the English Catholic Aristocracy by *Julia Camoys Stonor*

I saw Satan On The Northern Line by *Nick Awde*

Tattooing Arts of Tribal Women by *Lars Krutak*

Tattooed Mountain Women and Spoon Boxes of Daghestan: Magic Medicine Symbols in Silk, Stone, Wood and Flesh by *Robert Chenciner, Gabib Ismailov & Magomedkhan Magomedkhanov*

Mellotron: The Machine and the Musicians that Revolutionised Rock

Singer-Songwriters, Volume 1: Dave Cousins, Iain Matthews, Ralph McTell, Al Stewart, Richard Thompson

THE PUBLIC SCHOOL CHRONICLES:
  Vol. 1: **The Virgin Killers**
  Vol. 2: **An Overseas Boy**
  Vol. 3: **Blood Confession**

First published in 2011
by

Desert♥Hearts
www.deserthearts.com

PO BOX 2131
London W1A 5SU
England

© John Christopher Wilson 2011

Typeset and designed by Desert♥Hearts

ISBN 978-1-898948-07-0

The right of John Christopher Wilson to be identified as the author of this work has been asserted by him in accordance with the Copyright, Designs and Patents Act 1988.

All right reserved. No part of this publication may be reproduced, stored in or introduced into a retrieval system, or transmitted, in any form, or by any means (electronic, mechanical, photocopying, recording or otherwise) without the prior written permission of the publisher. Any person who does any unauthorized act in relation to this publication may be liable to criminal prosecution and civil claims for damages.

A CIP catalogue record for this book is available from the British Library.

Printed & bound by
Marksprint/Zrinski

Canto I

Dear B,

I pen this letter to you my friend,
Now my life's about to end,
You have shown me the greatest time
And proved that living can be sublime,
Now 'tis my duty to record our days:
The reckless joyance of your ways,
How to begin is hard to see,
Recalling how it used to be.

Routine is where I ought to start,
Train times and work that caged my heart,
I was a Commuter, you see,
My morning mule: The Six Fifty-Three,
Its thraldom I can scarce describe,
The collective boredom of a tribe,
For seven long years I rode that train,
I shudder to think upon it again.

The ceaseless search for a seat,
Linèd faces that oft repeat
Words into a mobile phone:
Their office talk, *my* silent groan,
Of course woe sometimes satisfies
As in the bash when a colleague dies,
Free booze and gossip at the wake
That thirst and grief equally slake.

So it was on The Six Fifty-Three,
Finding a seat gave secretive glee
And the presence of a pretty girl
Threw my feelings int' a whirl:
Her fiery mane and voluptuous top,
Luscious lips to make the heart stop
For a beat . . . and then accelerate,
My senses discombobulate!

But ever came the drudge of work,
The pointless grind of the office jerk,
In that cynical cycle I was included:
Making a diff'rence or simply deluded?
Every day was a Civil Service yawn
Till I began to wish I'd never been born
To serve such disingenuous masters,
Taking a dive for *their* lies and disasters.

So many projects I had that dragged,
My will to live fair waned and sagged,
Routine was lord of all I did,
Into auto-drive I languidly slid,
Every day proved the same slow drain:
A swig of coffee, catch the train,
Work, work, work and home for tea,
TV and bed by ten-thirty.

I was far from alone in my funk,
The whole nation was beset by junk,
Fuel cost a king's ransom,
Families huddled in one room,

Credit was a thing of the past,
A consumer dream that could not last,
Jobs were shed like no one cared,
The man on the bus was lost and scared.

The day we met I'd felt the strain
That morn as I got on the train,
The same tired or dozing faces,
The same jostling for too-few places,
Sadness of seeing make-up slapped on,
Besmirching a face till its beauty was gone,
And Unironed Shirtman with untied tie;
Sartorial shambles to make a grown man cry.

The under-dressed and the over-fed
And sick folk who should've stayed in bed,
The Pretty Girl was a dormant mystery,
Dreaming of love, oblivious of me?
It was Groundhog Day with a cruel twist:
If I'd died that day I would not have been missed,
My spirit was either banished or sleeping,
Rivulets of rain in sympathy weeping.

Then you did appear
To give me good cheer,
I watched you embark
As svelte as a lark,
Of windswept, erudite looks,
Man of Travel! Man of Books!
Your beauty gave me quite a fright,
I'd say I loved you at first sight.

The dopey and ugly commuter hoard
Continued to look jaded and bored,
As you glided 'twixt them through the carriage
They did not see the subtle marriage
Of grace and wisdom in your features,
They slumbered on: Oh, wretched creatures!
Except a girl opposite with a cough,
Who rose abruptly and got off.

You claimed her seat in a trice
With slickness that did swift suffice,
And beamed a special smile at me
Which those others failed to see,
I felt an urge to talk with you,
At first my words would not come through,
As the man beside me started yawning
I found my tongue and said—Good Morning.

—Good morning, came your reply,
—I believe the sun will soon come out,
—It'll be a day to behold the sky,
—Of its beauty there'll be no doubt,
—Sometimes I head into town and wonder why
—I've bothered, and turn about,
—Though not today for I'm in a hurry
—To see my publisher, Mr Murray.

You said you were a performer of rap
Touring widely while avoiding the trap
Of acting like a rapper all of the time
Or masquerading as a baron of crime,

You said your words would never cease
If you could be a prince of peace,
—As an artiste I'm named B-Zee,
—But call me B, it's easier, see.

You politely asked all about me,
I said I worked for the Ministry
Or The Department as it is now known,
Its usefulness shrinking as its size has grown,
I told you I fixed things for the Minister
While being discreet about the sinister
Aspect of my daily bind,
You nodded sagely; you didn't mind.

Our words flowed like a mountain stream,
You talked of travel as if in a dream,
It made me yearn to tag along
But I was no *Free Bird* of the song,
Besides I'd lose my Honours List mention
And final salary government pension,
Too soon the train reached Victoria Station,
I had so enjoyed our conversation!

—Goodbye, I said as we left the train,
—I suppose I shan't see you again,
—It's been a great pleasure to meet,
—A joy and a commuter's treat,
—I sincerely wish you all the best,
—I'm sure you're a cut above the rest
—Of the rap stars on our Earth,
—You were rapping, I'd wager, at birth!

You said—You are too kind, my friend,
—I could use a fellow like you,
—Our time together need not end,
—We'd taste adventure before we're through,
—On that you *surely* could depend,
—I'd say your life would feel brand new,
—If money's a worry, it's no object,
—Think it over before you reject.

I confess I was tempted by this madness,
My commuter's life gave me sadness,
I felt frozen alive in an ice cube
And my girl had dumped me on the Tube
As we'd set off for a break in Scotland,
Why Lorraine did it I'll never understand,
But despite my deep and unrelenting pain
Could I quit for a stranger on the train?

—I can see, you surmised—You are unsure,
—That's wise; I will say goodbye,
—You have a good job; who'd ask for more?
—It is not for me to question why,
—You I shall no longer bore,
—We must part; the tide is high,
—But if perchance you have a change of heart,
—Here this time next week our voyage will start.

So I shook his hand at our parting,
Little knowing my life was re-starting,
Was there a certain spring in my gait
As I reported for work eight minutes' late?

The Minister wanted a re-messaged speech,
Its insincerity made me beseech:
—For a change, let's tell the truth!
He stared at me as though uncouth.

Next day a buff envelope awaited me
When I reached the office from The Six Fifty-Three,
I tore it open without delay or fear,
But what it said from my eye rent a tear,
After my long service to government,
On my way I was to be sent
Along with a hundred and ten others;
Loyal breadwinners, fathers and mothers.

My boss *Dog Breath* said—You can take us to a tribunal!
—But it won't match the cash we're offering you,
(I didn't meet the Minister again,
He never learnt to take his shame
Though his wily ways wouldn't set him free:
His black heart failed him, aged fifty-three),
The next week found me at platform's end,
You grinned and said—Let's go, my friend!

The Brighton train proved pleasant and fast
With wine we toasted the death of my past,
—I trust, you said—you've brought your passport,
—Yes, I replied—I'll not be caught short,
You said you'd like to call me Cam:
—I want you to be my Main Man,
—You will be my MC C,
—I shall be your MC B.

The Captain was waiting at the station
And drove us in a state of elation
To Brighton Marina to board your boat;
An ancient sailing ship of note,
You whispered—It's manned by a top crew
—But we give the orders, me and you!
I asked—B, why did you choose me?
You smiled—Let's call it destiny!

The sun shone bright as hope that day,
Our tongues had silver words to say,
We knocked back Champagne on the deck
And joked our lives were but a wreck,
You told me about your former wife
Who'd caught you out to twist the knife,
I opened my heart on my ladette Lorraine
Whose sudden flight had caused me such pain.

—Don't fret, you said—It's no big deal!
—It happens to someone every day,
—What is love? When is it real?
—What does it mean to have your way?
—A man needs more than sex, I feel,
—Don't give 'em their oats too soon I say!
—So many young women entice you to bed
—Having pledged their heart to another instead.

I said with this I fully concurred,
—Some girls took *laddish* to the absurd,
—Lorraine had displayed her builder's crack
—And Maori tattoos upon her back,

—An ancient moped she rode unstable
—And easy drank me under the table,
—My arty chums she liked to offend,
—They nicknamed her *my 'boyfriend'!*

B, you said you fully understood,
With girls you knew not where you stood
You said—I was stalked by a girl, Caroline
—Who dressed like a boy and thought that was fine,
—Once in a temper she pulled a knife,
—But she was a breeze compared to my wife!
—Yet they say with me ladies shouldn't go
—Because I'm mad, bad and dangerous to know!

Suddenly you were melancholy
As if you pondered on past folly,
You said—In truth, I didn't treat her well,
—My belovèd ex-wife Annabelle,
—I was too fond of my half-sister,
—It proved quite futile to resist her,
—I'd compare my two loves in my head,
—Likewise, rashly, in my bed!

For a moment we sat in silent reverie,
A mental picture danced betwixt us merrily,
Presently I said—There are no laws,
—About the place where true love falls!
You smiled about your little slip,
And said—Let's stroll about the ship
—And draw up our future plans,
—Prepare for fun, Commuterman!

We were already well out to sea,
A fair distance from dear Blighty,
I was impressed by the vessel's size
And its blackened timbers worldly wise,
The ship was oaken and clinker-built,
The crew sailed her fast, at jaunty tilt,
You said you'd bought her for old times' sake:
—*The Bolivar's* historic and no mistake.

—My friend, I found myself sigh,
—What *are* we doing, you and I?
—Maybe I'm running from the Credit Crunch
—But there's no such thing as a free lunch,
—I must somehow pay my due,
—What would you like me to do?
—Just name it and I'll give it a go,
—I'm sure my worth will quickly show.

You said—My dear Cam, I daresay
—You will aid and abet me in many a way,
—Tell me first your favourite tunes,
—The sounds that make you skit your spoons!
My pop knowledge was no cop at all,
My youth was misspent inside Whitehall
But a thought occurred in my adversity:
—I did some DJ-ing at university.

You said—Now I start to comprehend
—Why you are *right* through and through
—My every issue to amend
—And sticky problems to eschew,

—Because I must have a DJ to attend
—To my gigs; it shall be you!
—I'll teach you the decks to meanly mix,
—You'll drive them wild, those hot-pant chicks!

My DJ-ing schooling commenced that day,
My friend taught me just what to play,
And to segue tunes from his collection,
I was tutored to near-perfection,
All the time we sailed along,
Enjoying nights of wine and song,
A blitheful present the memory mars,
On deck we lolled 'neath a canvas of stars.

Our adventure, you said, had only begun,
First stop: the coolest club in the sun,
You said—We'll make a Lisbon packet,
—Euro hip-hop's a wondrous racket,
I said I hoped I'd hit the mark:
—It's well moved on, this DJ-ing lark,
You said—Don't be *too* good, MC C,
—I'd rather you didn't upstage me!

The weather changed like night to day,
A storm struck us in the Bay of Biscay,
The masts creaked beside mountainous waves,
I feared we were headed for watery graves,
You took the helm on the brine-lashed deck,
I cowered in my cabin, a dog-sick wreck,
By foulest weather we were bevelled and worn
Till we eyed Portugal in the rising morn.

We breakfasted like kings on the foredeck,
Bilious I felt but what the heck!
You said—Build your strength, my boy,
—Eat your fill and don't be coy,
—In Lisbon you mustn't show the strain
—If called on to go like an express train!
I chuckled—B, you are a schemer
—As sure as I'm an incurable dreamer.

The ocean gleamed iridescent blue,
I felt happy through and through,
My strength returned to me by the second
With a vigour for which I'd not reckoned,
We swam in the sea alongside the boat,
—Warmer than the Hellespont, I heard you note,
Your graceful power inspired my every limb,
—Cam, you said—I love a little swim.

That evening we threw a party,
All of us were hale and hearty,
As a token of thanks we cooked for the crew:
Spicy fish in a tureen of stew
Washed down by beer and wine,
Under a treacle moon like a blessèd sign,
The Mate played accordion into the night,
Merry we danced until the sky grew light.

This, B, is my letter's forty-second verse,
Forty-two, the answer to the Universe,
Certainly I'd never felt such felicity,
Our lives together: a fine complicity,

Sometimes I'd think of expenses and lies,
The greed and hypocrisy that'd offended my eyes,
All I'd fled when I ditched my computer
And my sad former life as a London commuter.

Did I miss East Croydon station's clarty plastic
Where feckless youths flashed knicker elastic?
Or singleton women out on the snog
Trawling West End bars, kissing many a frog?
I didn't; I swear I did not
Miss any of it one solitary jot,
London could keep its August without a peep of sun
And last-train *Go Large Whoppers* in a greasy bun.

Soon in Lisbon we did dock,
I felt certain this town we'd rock,
I saw the crowd gathered on the quay,
Waiting, nay, clamouring for you, B,
I knew our show couldn't fail to be hot
Whether I DJ-ed a storm or not,
Here you were the star all right
And gladly I basked in your limelight.

The gig that night was in a vast tavern,
A cross between a club and a cavern,
In hoards your fevered fans surged in,
Nervously I waited for my set to begin,
I spun the discs while brightly beaming,
My arms ablaze, my fingers steaming,
The dance floor became one body sweating like a
    shower,

The crowd was going wild... then I lost all power.

A plug I'd pulled out through inexperience,
It took me some moments to recommence,
I mixed some classic grooves into an anthem new,
Something I couldn't have done if it wasn't for you
And all you had taught me aboard the ship,
The crowd quickly forgave my clumsy slip
Going crazy for my music in every sense,
When I announced you, their cheers were immense.

I put on your track and you took to the stage,
Your rap songs were witty, their meanings sage,
In the palm of your hand the audience was held,
You took risks unparalleled,
Your gentleman's manners had belied
The risqué humour lurking inside,
Transfixed was I as you wowed the floor,
I felt I loved you all the more.

Like a carpet seller without his rugs
Or a junkie bereft of drugs,
I realised I'd be lost without you,
You'd given me far more than you knew,
That evening was a revelation
Which climaxed in a celebration,
Each of us was joined by a beauty that night,
And enjoyed their loving until first light.

I slept like a log long into the day,
At what time I awoke I couldn't say,

The bed was empty save for me,
No sign of my girl remained to see,
I thought—Did it happen, that loving supreme?
It started to feel like another damp dream,
But how we'd made love so smoothly
Replayed in my head like a cheesy blue movie.

In the spacious flat that we had hired
I found you in the kitchen looking tired,
—Hello Cameron, you said
—Fresh from your debauchèd bed,
—I've been challenged to a Death Slam
—By Lisbon's maddest rapper, a parlous man,
—He called to say tonight he will take my life;
—Your girl is his sister; mine is his wife!

—Blimey O'Reilly! I said,
—Get this wrong and we'll be dead,
—Don't panic, said you—I'll win hands down,
—I'm the Daddy in this one-horse town,
—But we shouldn't have loved those girls into a trance
—Without first checking out their provenance,
—Though, perhaps, loving so rich in spice
—Is bound to come at a hefty price.

B, you smiled warmly at me
With a knowing glint that set me free,
I trusted you that it'd be OK
And we'd live to see another day,
Besides at sorting out crises I had flair,

I'd buried the Minister's lewd affair
And from the media managed to hide
The time he'd groped an intern's backside.

At the club that night rumour was rife,
You could've cut the air with a knife,
The Wolf had challenged the legendary B,
To a Death Slam; there'd be blood to see,
Young women were frisky with violence so near,
Men more tense; the joint was laced with fear,
I overheard one say—The Wolf will gun B down,
—This time he's gone too far, that lousy English
 clown.

I played the tunes but could not fill the floor,
Few were in the mood with danger at the door,
All eyes were on The Wolf as he entered with his
 crew,
Shocked by the cheering, I turned to look at you,
B, you were cooler than an Alpine snow-cap
While I was nervous, in a desperate flap,
When my fade-out was almost gone,
You said to me—Bring the Wolf-man on!

Trembling, I read my script in the harsh spotlight,
—Ladies and Gentlemen, we've a treat for you
 tonight:
—The most deadly slam ever to be put on:
—The British B versus The Wolf of Lisbon,
—They'll rap their hearts out for your delight,
—In a war of words, a mortal fight,

—You'll decide by your hue and cry
—Who will live and who will die.

—Wolf has two minutes to set out his case,
—B-Zee then responds to save his face,
—After each man, the crowd makes its feelings known,
—The noise level you produce is on a meter shown,
—Tonight's umpire, the owner of this club
—Reads out the results and herein lies the rub,
—The victor basks in the glory of his art
—And shoots the loser through the heart.

I had nearly finished the script you'd penned for me
And knew that evening might be the last you'd see,
Despite our secret plan, your prospects were poor,
For all your pluck and wit, your corpse could hit the floor,
With a few words to read before I was done
A hush bound the crowd listening as one,
On stage you held Wolf in a glare intense,
Voice cracking, I proclaimed—Let battle commence!

If Wolf was nervous it didn't make him hesitate,
Featly and grinning, he stepped up to the plate,
His bandana bore the skull and crossbones,
Many photos were taken on mobile phones,
A silence followed as deep as a black hole
Like a bottomless cave without a living soul,
Wolf stared you straight in the eye
And said—Englishman, prepare to die

—For committing a heinous crime,
—You sackless bag of British slime,
—Don't try to treat me as a wittol,
—You sorry excuse for a sh't'ole,
—I won't ignore what you did to my wife,
—I'll gut you alive with my rustiest knife,
—And with my sister your friend had his fun
—Little knowing what he had begun.

—I spit on you, my rapper foe,
—Your life is over, I think you know,
—Death must come to you and yours:
—Toilet traders, English whores!
—I'll toast the day I meet your *mudda*
—And do my worst to your *brudda*
—As your sister is captured by my men,
—You'll be lucky to see her again.

—Think me a monster but it's an eye for an eye,
—You laughed out loud as you made my girls cry,
—Cigar smoke you blew in their faces
—And mistreated them in private places,
—My belovèd wife you threatened to kill
—You said—Sleep with me or write your will,
—Your Main Man filmed it all; I bet
—To sell it on the internet.

—So brothers and sisters learn the truth
—About the guest beneath our roof,
—The scuzzy, vile, dirty dastard,
—Venal and filthy minded b'stard,

—My good and virtuous Lisbon throng,
—You can tell what's right from wrong,
—Scream and boo and chant, I say,
—So I may blow this beast away.

I was shattered by his lies,
Yet they drew the people's cries
And bays for you to swiftly die,
The meter's needle shot sky high,
The Club Owner perused the sickly dial,
Which didn't look promising by a mile,
I sensed that our lives were on the line
As he said—Wolf's score is Nine Point Nine.

It felt like a shadow appearing on my lung,
I knew our song was almost sung,
Lisbon Mob like Lisbon Man,
They wanted us to carry the can,
Letting Wolf's hemlock into their minds trickle,
How could they be so weak and fickle?
I thought—Last night you'd held them in your spell
—But now they'd send you straight down to Hell.

A fallen hero, a figure of hate,
Your turn had come your case to state,
I feared you'd have just minutes left alive
Unless I could help you to survive,
The crowd resembled a blood-crazed hound,
Wickedness closed in all around,
You faced death as calm as Charles the First,
Confounding evil as your words out burst.

—Lah-di-dah and rock-a-dock,
—Hi-di-Hi and diddly-dee,
—Chaka Khan and Shappi shock,
—Wacko Jacko and A-B-C,
—Oscar Wilde said—Soda and Hock!
—Growing on a pasta tree!
—All of this makes more sense,
—Than The Wolf-man's evidence.

—You've heard the claims of me he's made,
—That I'm a kidnapper, a sadist as well,
—That your kindness I've repaid
—By plighting your lovely women hell,
—Chaining and wounding in a sick cockade,
—Defiling their bodies for video to sell,
—My dear friends, *none* of this is true,
—How could I do it, when I love you?

—I shall confess what we *did* do,
—Last night we fell for these girls' charms
—And loved them tender the whole night through
—With passion that invigorates, not harms,
—Mine taught me tricks *I* never knew,
—We were an enlacement of legs and arms,
—With great passion each girl cried out,
—From their husbands they'd had nowt!

And so, B, Stanza Sixty-Nine I come to write,
This number seems quite apposite,
You were telling of the loving that we'd had,
With other men's wives, we'd been bad,

Though legitimate; it was their decision,
The girls had acted of their own volition,
Your peroration was nearing its end,
You summed up the case our lives to defend:

—The Wolf's claims beggar belief,
—I've never caused a lady pain,
—I'd rather be a lowly thief
—Than harm a woman; that's insane!
—Wolf is lying through his teeth,
—He must have water on the brain,
—Shout and cheer and yell for me,
—Tell the world who should walk free.

Lisbon's women screamed their lungs out,
Of your innocence they had no doubt,
They knew those girls slept around,
With countless lovers they'd been found,
But the menfolk much less desired
To make the noise that you required,
They feared that if they saved you that night,
They'd meet the Wolf's flick-knife in a fight.

The needle swung across the dial,
I watched its progress for a while,
It seemed high, though not quite there,
The Owner betrayed a troubled stare,
He shook his head and I thought—Feck,
—Now we're headed for a wreck,
With resigned eyes he read the score:
—Mr B has Nine Point Four!

My heart was banging drum and bass
As I slid so slyly into place,
All eyes were focused on you, my friend,
Could sweet heaven your death forfend?
—I'm afraid, said Wolf—This is the end of your fun,
As in time with his crew he drew his gun,
You said—Before you shoot, tell me why
—You're *really* so keen for me to die?

The Wolf scoffed and said—OK
—Though I'm going to kill you anyway,
—You know I had to win our slam last year,
—To pay off debts I'd run up here,
—When you beat me, hope went limp
—In desperation I became a pimp,
—But a judge locked me up in the shank,
—For that stretch of bird, I've you to thank.

Some girls booed but it was too late,
The Death Slam had sealed your fate,
From side-stage I could see Wolf snigger,
As his finger played upon the trigger,
In one fell swoop I cut the power
And set off the alarms and sprinkler shower,
Of your presence beside me I was aware,
Like bats from Hell we got out of there!

Down the steps to the corridor,
You whisked me to a tradesman's door,
—Well done, old boy, you said to me,
Somehow in the dark you could see,

We heard gunshots above; Oh brother!
Wolf's gang were shooting each other,
Outside, the Captain and Mate awaited on scooters,
They drove us to safety sounding their hooters.

People scattered as we rode like no tomorrow,
Our time in the city had been tinged with sorrow,
Back on the ship we swiftly anchored away,
I was more relieved than I could say,
We watched the land retreat from the deck,
After all that'd happened I felt like a wreck,
I said—I trust it's not like this every time,
—Perhaps, you teased—we should toe the line!

We sailed at a rate of knots into the starry dark,
Trying to recuperate from our Lisbon lark,
The crew regaled us with their high jinks,
Enjoying the night life with plenty of drinks
On their famous runs ashore,
Kissing young ladies and much more,
And of a speakeasy you would not believe:
A club to die for whilst on leave.

We joshed away like fast friends do,
And told our story fair and true,
The men received it with the greatest mirth,
Rolling with laughter for all they were worth,
At the tale's end, you proposed a toast
To the people who had helped us most:
Our loyal crew who saved our bacon
Without whom we'd have been forsaken.

Port and rum we sank by the cask
And got exceedingly drunk as was our task,
Few would question that we succeeded,
Our consumption went unimpeded,
The Cook walked upon his hands
Before regaling us with yarns from fabled lands
Of love and exotic trysts, heaven sent,
We all knew exactly what he meant.

Overwhelmed was I by sheer exhaustion,
The action we'd seen was out of proportion
To our brief sojourn in that pleasant land,
More excitement than a man could stand,
My every muscle and sinew did ache,
Perhaps quitting London had been a mistake,
Sozzled, I slurred—Where will this end, B?
—Dear boy, you enthused—Sweet Italy!

The next few days were an oasis of peace
Although my flashbacks still didn't cease,
I thought back to my occasional caper
With girls I had met through a free newspaper,
The ads I'd placed when feeling *lovestruck*,
The many let-downs and random luck,
I'd become a blind-date love junkie,
A phase that'd proved neither fun nor funky.

Often I'd drink cider on the train,
A booze trenchcoat for my mental pain
And abject failure to find a soulmate;
I'd even tried to lose some weight,

But the real problem was inside of me,
The Minister's stooge I'd plumped to be,
I had chosen to act as that egotist's tool,
The trusting public to befool.

I thought then of what Lorraine would say
If she could see me on that princely day
Heading the helm of this grand ship,
Setting the course without a slip,
A wondrous *joie de vivre* I had found
Since she'd dumped me on The Underground,
How I would enjoy telling my ex-lover
That the sliding doors had closed on *her*!

For a fortnight we sailed on our way,
Sun soaking us glorious day after day,
You said—We're headed for my special place,
—Where I first found my true space:
An isle as mystic green as one could wish to see,
An idyll where we can breathe, you and me,
It's a spot where volcanic rocks smoulder
And history's perched upon your shoulder.

Despite all that we had done
My former life had still not gone,
What would it take to erase
The lurching wraith of yesterdays?
I thought of Amy Trolley-Girl on the train,
My love for her had been insane,
In the morning she'd serve me tea,
By night: *Strongbow* and sympathy.

I pondered those foolhardy times,
My puerile habits and gentle crimes,
—You're caught in a trap, a mate had joked,
But it was true; to my work I'd been yoked,
Now my existence was an exploration,
I'd waved goodbye to desperation,
You pointed out the beguiling skyline
And a shimmering island that looked divine.

It was by no means the first isle we'd seen,
But by far the most startling, serene;
An emerald gem in a turquoise sea,
Its beauty a gift for posterity,
Or at least that was how it was painted
By you in words poetic, untainted,
I could not but concur
As I took in Kefalonia.

—We're here at last, you said to me,
—I'm sure you'll love this isle,
—It is where I feel most free,
—Here people find their inner style,
—Gigging on the beach we'll be,
—Raising the bar by a mile,
—But if you want the party to begin
—Don't bring along a mandolin!

In the capacious harbour we did moor
And rowed our tender to the shore,
Again your spirits were sky high,
I could not help but wonder why

This place gave such a charge to you,
You looked as if you were brand new,
The sun was bright; the breeze balmy and cool
At our Roman villa, replete with a pool.

—This is it, my favourite home,
Said you—My heart sings here,
—When I return whence I roam,
—These verdant woods renew my cheer
—Like the snowy peaks and lighthouse dome,
—And tomorrow on stage we'll appear
—On a beach resembling a fjord
—Where we shall reap our just reward.

You regaled me with your lavish plans:
A month of shows upon the sands,
Tickets had been sold wide and far,
Revellers were pouring in for your hurrah,
To name your co-stars you could scarce begin,
Even Fat Boy Slim was flying in,
But you and I would top the bill,
Even now I can feel the thrill!

You said—Tonight at eight there'll be a party
—Thrown by the Mayor, it should be hearty,
—The women on this isle are divine,
—Worthy of a votive shrine,
I warned—We *must* behave well
—Or we'll be back in bad-boy hell!
Said you—At my expense you make merry,
—My conduct will be exemplary!

We laughed and to a cove we slipped
And shed our clothes and skinny-dipped,
Diving deeply into the sea,
Swimming in tandem, utterly free,
We dawdled back to the villa and ate
And dressed up for our evening date,
Golden rays covered the island like a blanket
As we made our entrance at the mayoral banquet.

The party proved a lavish affair,
I felt elated just to be there,
On the balcony Champagne cocktails were drunk
And many a gin and tonic was sunk,
The Mayor seemed a charming chap,
And even said he loved your rap,
You took his praise in your stride;
A content man of quiet pride.

I own it was I who let us down,
I, a mere drear of London town,
Beyond a shadow of doubt it was my fault,
My emotions, though, were hard to halt,
I tried to check them, I swear I did,
When *she* flirted with me, I should've hid,
She sweetly spoke and enticingly smiled,
By the soirée's end, I was beguiled.

At the time it seemed so right
To make a friend that starry night,
You did not pay it any mind,
When the *craic* is good, all are blind

And how could we possibly foreknow
A twist as strange as August snow?
Did I display mere innocence
Or just a dearth of common sense?

Athina was my new love's name,
To great beauty she could lay claim,
We just exchanged numbers on that occasion,
Nothing more despite our elation,
I invited her to our first gig date,
She said that she could hardly wait,
The start of something magical, I dreamed,
The girl I'd been waiting for, or so it seemed.

In a month of gigs upon the beach,
We made them dance and saw them reach
New peaks of joy; What a crowd!
They were awesome gigs; we did them proud!
Athina came every night, me to be near,
We became friends and lovers dear,
Her jet black eyes and long brown hair
Always gave me thoughts I shall not share.

There was a carnival atmosphere,
Nights of dancing, song and beer,
Athina said she was there for the season
On a break with her brother; who needs a reason?
I confessed to you, B, I was in love,
You chuckled and said—Heavens above!
—Sounds like your heart has AWOL gone,
—I'm thrilled for you, dear Cameron.

Your habits though were dissolute,
That month you plucked so much young fruit,
You liked to have them two by two,
One girl was not enough for you,
I wasn't jealous of your flaw,
I was with Athina and wanted no more,
But as your wingman I sometimes acted instead
Feeding in lines to help you lure girls to bed.

The crew was also having a halcyon time,
Making the most of our party sublime,
Stories of our men's exploits abounded,
Their antics across the island resounded,
No one minded, it was honest fun,
No need this time for us to run,
Weighing anchor would be at *our* choosing
When we decided to return to cruising.

Our final gig was a *tour de force*,
I played and you rapped until you were hoarse,
The crowd was loved-up and ecstatic,
Trance-dancing on automatic,
Afterwards I helped you bag one last brace,
You promised each girl a *pearl necklace*,
Whilst with Athina I spent a lyrical night,
Loving her pure, good and right.

After she'd left the following morning
I found you in the atrium, luxuriantly yawning,
You said you were utterly replete,
Your girls had worn you out between the sheets:

—It's time for us to quit, my friend,
—Or our stay shall never end,
—Let's sail tonight while the going's good,
—Bring Athina if you think you should.

Once again you had read my mind,
I didn't want to leave her behind,
But would she want to sail with us
And join our sudden exodus?
I raced off to ask her if she'd come,
My heart was beating like a drum
Fearing she'd spurn me for another,
I found her talking with her brother.

B, you told me later he was a toe-rag:
A skull-faced, lying, no-good scumbag,
But my love for Athina was so great
I saw not her brother's heart of hate,
To me he seemed a low-key businessman;
An unremarkable also-ran,
So, I took Athina out to lunch,
That something was up she had a hunch.

—You have news to tell, I can see,
She very soon did say to me,
—Yes, I replied, choked up a mite,
—I'm leaving with my friend tonight,
—It's sudden, I realise, but please come along,
—We'll sail the seas, our hearts full of song,
—I know it's a lot, without notice, to ask,
—But, imagine, in ocean spray we would bask.

My love sighed deeply and stared at me,
Tears welled up in her eyes, I could see,
I feared at once that she'd say no
And to sea without her I'd have to go
Or I'd have to choose between you, B,
And the girl who meant so much to me,
I was considering this position so rum
When to my relief she said—I'll come!

With those few words she'd banished my fears,
Overjoyed, I had to fight back the tears,
Embracing her, I said—My love,
—You've lifted me to heaven above,
—Join me at dusk on board the ship,
—From these shores we'll soundlessly slip
—And sail with the greatest felicity
—Towards the golden coast of Italy.

That last day passed so fast,
Our time ashore had been a blast,
We stowed our chattels upon the boat
Plus your new purchase, a billy goat,
You bade fond farewell to many a girl,
The isle's women were in a whirl,
By the time their kisses and tears were through,
I thought—Who *hasn't* given their heart to you?

Nobody was more surprised than me
To be the one taking a lover to sea,
She'd keep me young while I was away,
Loving me tender by night and day,

I felt that seeing her walk on board
Would be my greatest possible reward,
However as the sun went down
There was no sign of her in town.

Even you looked a tad concerned
As my face red with anxiety burned,
—Don't worry, you said—I daresay you'll find,
—We're not going to leave Athina behind,
I gulped audibly and forced back a tear,
My mouth was dry; my mind full of fear,
After Lorraine could I take the pain
Of being ditched all over again?

At last in the distance Athina appeared,
The crowd ship-side applauded and cheered,
It was as if the whole island shared my joy;
The glorious sight of my darling ahoy,
But something inside me started to shrink,
My hopes and dreams began to sink,
For a voyage she did not look ready,
All she carried was a giant, pink teddy.

—Thank God you're here, I said,
On the quay to her and ted,
—I thought we might have to sail without you,
—Which is more than I could bear to do,
She burst into tears as she proclaimed:
—Cam, I can't come, I feel so ashamed,
—My brother was livid that I wanted to leave,
—The rage he flew into you would not believe.

—We'll talk to him, I said to her,
—And soon I'm sure he will concur,
—No, don't do that, she begged of me,
—Go now; I'll join you in Italy,
—Next month I'm due to visit friends there,
—We'll be together then, I swear,
—Their daughter's very sick; please be humane
—And take her this teddy bear before we meet again.

I was left confused by this spurious yarn;
As love-blind as the conquests of *Don Juan*,
I'm sure you'd have posed her a question or two
But held back 'cause you knew my feelings were true,
I kissed Athina and took the weighty teddy,
Once back on board we were ready,
Sailing that night I'd never felt lonelier,
Leaving my heart on Kefalonia.

For a week I remained a molten mess,
The grief at my loss I couldn't redress,
You tried everything to lift my mood:
The finest wines, the richest food,
I'm sure you knew that I'd been dumped,
My self-confidence had taken a shunt,
And every time I felt more steady,
I caught sight of the mocking teddy.

The goat you'd bought ran amok,
Life at sea doesn't suit livestock,
He found everything we could stow
Rummaging for grazing down below,

We called him Elvis and he joined Captain's Table,
I slipped him scraps whenever I was I able,
But then one unforgettable night
We discovered Elvis as high as a kite.

He was rock 'n' rolling like The King,
I swear dear Elvis was trying to sing,
—Hey, I joshed—What's with the *Jailhouse Rock*?
—You're off your trolley, my old cock,
You, B, laughed louder and louder:
—The goat's been on the marching powder,
You said, finding the teddy with its side split
Bags of cocaine gushing from it.

When I saw that scene I started to quiver,
Athina had sold me down the river,
She was using me as her drugs mule,
I could have wept; I'd been such a fool!
She must have known what was in the teddy
But for the truth I wasn't ready,
Shocked, I said—I've been betrayed,
You put your arm around me and looked dismayed.

I hid the cocaine under my bunk
Saying to Elvis—You've had enough junk!
We discussed just what to do
In a sombre meeting with the crew,
For me they were full of sympathy,
No one showed a hint of glee,
We agreed that overboard the cocaine we'd throw,
But you said—Before we do, let's give it a go!

Into mad hours of drug abuse we dived,
I scarcely know how we survived,
Cocaine we snorted for supper and dinner,
At this druggie lark I was a beginner,
I felt like The Ruler of the Universe,
At a thousand miles an hour, mind teeming with verse,
Before that crazy night was over
We'd all experienced a *Supernova*.

At dawn you chucked the rest into the drink,
Five kilos of cocaine began to sink
And dissolved rapidly betwixt Greece and Italy
Giving Neptune a high leagues beneath the sea,
Though it was tempting to keep a private supply
We believed you when you said we would surely die
If we repeated our drugs fiesta over and over
Ignoring the warning of our cocaine hangover.

We tried to fall back into the ship's routine,
That night now seemed a Class A dream,
After the drugs we'd so readily imbued,
Even Elvis the Goat acted subdued,
Sore-headed, we talked about the teddy,
And how, with revenge, we ought to be ready
To pay Athina and her brother back for the trick
    they'd played,
To make them suffer, a cunning plan we laid.

I said—Let's not give the teddy to Athina's *friends*,
She must come in person to make amends,
—I'll text her to say only she can receive it,

—Writing—I miss you so much you wouldn't believe
    it,
You said—It's a sound plan without a doubt,
—And it should smoke these rascals out,
—They'll fly to Italy to retrieve their coke,
—We'll fill Teddy with flour for a joke!

I said—Yes, and demand one hundred grand,
—They'll cough up to get their drugs back in hand,
—We should say we know what's inside,
—It's true; we hardly would have lied,
—When all's been said and done
—We want to have a little fun,
—I loved Athina but after the stunt she's pulled,
—It's her turn now to be befooled.

And, so, the scene was set,
You and I had cast our net,
With a text I laid the bait
Stressing Athina must not be late,
I had to take the utmost care
To ensure she would be there,
We knew her brother wouldn't be far away,
The rabid, cloying, canine stray!

Ravenna was the chosen rendezvous,
A town that meant so much to you,
You said we'd lodge in an apartment there
With a devoted woman, sensuous and fair,
I joshed—You've a girl in every port,
—Well, I'm a sailor, was your retort,

I said—Ravenna seems a fitting place
—To sort out this business face to face.

A leisurely course we plotted
And to it a full week allotted,
You said—Let's give them all the time they need
—To turn up there to sate their greed,
I warned—Her brother could be armed,
—This time we might not leave unharmed,
You said—We can handle that wild rover,
—Let's tool up and do him over!

You led me down into the galley
And yanked the fridge into the alley
To raise a plank by a sunken hook
Revealing a cache of guns of deadly look:
Pistols and semi-automatic weapons,
A toolkit fit for mafia dons,
I stared and thought—I'm in too deep,
—The road to Hell is short and steep!

Sleepless that night in my berth,
I thought how little my life was worth,
A single shot could stub it out,
I was in peril, there was no doubt,
And if I killed a man I'd die of shame,
Would Lady Luck spare my good name?
I began to consider our entire plan
A jape worthy of Desperate Dan!

In the morning, you sensed I was of troubled mind,

You said—I guess our hangover made us blind,
—I'd say our plan's not quite right
—And we could do without this fight,
—Pride comes before a fall,
—This showdown makes no sense at all,
—For a needless battle I'm not ready,
—Let's sail to Venice and feck their teddy!

Soon our course had been reset,
—A mere tilt of the tiller, you said—No sweat,
—Now we're on our way to Venice town
—Where jeroboams of champers we shall down,
—I'll take a canal-side mansion like in the old days,
—And revisit my carefree, sportive ways,
—The Film Festival's coming up,
—We'll bag some starlets with any luck.

The date of the Ravenna assignation passed,
That day I'd feared would be our last,
Venice was only a few hours' sail away,
You said—We'll settle in; then we'll play!
But that night we were awoken by a yell,
Unleashed above us were hounds of Hell,
We jumped up but downward were slammed,
The ship by pirates was being rammed.

—Get the guns, you sharpish said,
Too late! A muzzle was pointed at my head,
The rogues took the ship with rapier speed
That our crew could scarce impede,
The Look-out had missed their approach,

Our security was quickly broached,
The pirates encountered Cook having a fag,
They slit his throat and watched him splutter and
    gag.

There were a score of them, armed to the teeth,
Your look of rage surpassed your grief,
They cuffed and bound us on the deck
Covered with blood from Cook's gaping neck,
—You'll pay for this, you told our foes,
—I'll slash you to ribbons from your head to your
    toes,
Their main man laughed in your face
Saying—Shut up, lippy, you've run your race!

We were chained *en masse* to the mast,
I wondered how long our ordeal would last,
First light came and the pirates changed course
While smoking our cigars and glugging our sauce,
What tortures awaited us, what saga of sighs?
It was all my fault; tears welled up in my eyes,
Is this what happens when you dream of being free
And give up your seat on the Six Fifty-Three?

At steering the ship the pirates proved adept,
Along a new course she obediently swept,
It seemed to me away from Venice
Taking us to a great new menace,
The pirates' powerful launch did follow,
The sight of its guns filled me with sorrow,
On the horizon a floating *gin palace* I could espy

And an image which made me want to cry.

On the top deck stood Athina but what made me shudder
Was seeing her hand entwined with that of her brother,
They were the cause of our mishap:
The brains behind our callous kidnap,
Now they'd sneer at our hapless state
And preside over our unhappy fate,
Still, I could not begin to understand
Why she appeared to be holding his hand.

At gunpoint the pirates finally untied us,
Warning—You're fish food if you make a fuss,
The gin palace was anchored and we moored alongside,
To its gaudy bulk our grand ship was tied,
You whispered to me—Don't lose your nerve,
—We *will* triumph, with daring and verve,
When Athina and her brother stepped aboard
I prayed to God—Help us, O Lord!

We huddled together, girded by the pirate crew,
Athina's Brother made a beeline for you,
Shouting—Rapper Boy, where's my chuffing teddy?
You said—Down below, I'll show you when you're ready,
But a pirate produced it with its girth still open wide,
We hadn't got round to putting flour inside,
The Brother's face turned crimson as he went insane,
—Tell me, you b'stards, where is my cocaine?

B, you scoffed with reckless scorn:
—You're in danger of making me yawn,
—We enjoyed your gift; it put us in the pink
—And when our party ended, the rest went in the drink,
—We planned to confront you but changed our mind,
—I guess we had tired of mixing with your kind,
—Now you're trespassing here, getting up my nose,
—You couldn't just p'ss off home, I suppose?

Spurred on by your courage, I rounded on Athina,
Saying—I loved you but what could be obscener
—Than the way you've betrayed me?
—I look at you now and despise what I see,
—Minutes ago you were holding hands with your brother,
—As if he in kisses you longed to smother.
She said—He's not my brother, he's my boyfriend,
—I'm sorry, Cam, but our fling had to end.

The Brother sneered—You don't even know my name,
—You British fools with brains so lame,
—In these parts I'm known as *The Ram*,
—The King of Sex and Drugs I am,
—Cam, I allowed you to knock off my girl for free,
—The least you could do was a coke run for me,
The Ram turned to the pirates and said—What say you
—That for stealing our gear, we scourge these two?

The pirates' roar of approval was vast,
You and I were tied either side of the mast,
Cheek by jowl we'd take our punishment,
Flesh from our backs would be raked and rent,
The Ram produced a scourge oiled for duty,
—A tri-thonged leather whip, he bragged—of Biblical beauty,
—A dozen lashes from this will loosen your tongue,
—You'll sing like a canary when you're hamstrung.

Our shirts were stripped off and salt rubbed on our skin,
The Ram laughed—It'll hurt all the more when the lashes cut in,
—But we can stop now if you say where you've stashed my coke,
—Think carefully: this scourge will be no joke,
—It's going to be agony and don't forget
—Better men have died from what you'll get,
You spat—You've already murdered my dear Cook,
—For that, Ram, I'll hang you like mutton from a hook.

The Ram thrashed the scourge across your back with his full strength,
I felt the mast rock as the thongs ravaged down their length,
Again and again he struck, determined you should die,
Suffering so wistfully, you barely breathed a sigh,
Six, seven, eight strokes, blood streaming from your back,

An evil grimace on his face, he was cutting you no slack,
At nine strokes, Athina cried out—That's enough!
—If you kill him, we will never know where he
 stashed our stuff.

Reluctantly, The Ram put down his scourge of hate,
—Hang in there, B, I said, praying it was not too
 late,
I could not survive the thrashing you'd just taken,
If something didn't change, hope would be forsaken,
I prayed to the Virgin Mary for her intervention
And what swiftly then occurred defied all convention,
As The Ram your bonds roughly cut,
A crazed Elvis appeared and bit him on the butt!

I wrenched myself free, though smashing my watch,
Swinging round to kick The Ram in the crotch,
Elvis the Goat had a good gnash at it too
As the pirates were set upon by our brave crew,
Two of our number in the fighting were shot
After a string of buccaneers their just desserts got,
I went berserk after picking up the scourge,
Raking their bodies, pirate smirks I purged.

Despite your injuries from lashes of the whip,
You fought like a tiger to reclaim the ship,
A gun you seized and shot a pirate through the heart,
With a second round you blew another's brains
 apart,
The Ram tried to punch me but I lashed his face;
His good looks by a weeping wound replaced,

Athina hurried to help him off *The Bolivar*
Saying—This time, my lover, we've gone too far.

I shouted—Stop, you won't get away!
The Ram scoffed—Yeah, whatever you say,
Of Athina I asked—Why did you betray me?
She said—I'm amazed you cannot see,
—Despite the happy times together we spent,
—To you by my lover I was being sent,
—Though I must admit I came to love you
—And regret the hell I've put you through.

I felt cut up inside, as they slunk away
Down the gangplank to fight another day,
Some pirates fled in their launch; others stayed behind,
For those who remained, fate would prove unkind,
Athina rushed to pull up the anchor
And powered off with a look of rancour,
—Let's get after them, you said, but it was hopeless,
Our butcher's bill was high; the ship a bloody mess.

Half our crew were as-a-dodo dead,
The others wounded in trunk or head,
We'd make sure the remaining pirates came to a sticky end,
To Davy Jones' Locker their filthy souls we'd send,
I took you below deck to treat your graven back,
Shaking, I surveyed the carnage left by his attack,
I said—I'm sorry, this was my fault
—In falling for that wicked dolt.

—Nonsense, you said—How could you know?
—She looked as pure as virgin snow,
—We must live with a capital L,
—Even when it causes hell.
—You're too kind but what now? I said,
You replied—First we need to bury our dead
—And drink to them at a wake,
—We must not their memory forsake.

So we committed them to sea, shedding many a tear
And fortified ourselves with whisky and beer,
You lay on pillows on account of your pain,
I'd given you pills but your anguish was plain,
Just five of us were left alive, alas, alack,
We stayed on deck in case of further attack,
Such horror and violence obscene
Heralded, surely, the end of our dream.

We creaked onward into the dark,
My heart no longer into this lark,
I longed for London and the Six Fifty-Three;
The life where I had *not* been free,
I could see you were in a precarious state,
—Let's get you to hospital, I said—before it's too late,
—All right, you said—But I'll kill The Ram without a doubt,
—I am going to turn that scoundrel inside out!

During that long and harrowing night,
I weighed up the wrong against the right,

How could we stray so hideously far
From the people we really are?
I thought once more of my commuting time
And that honourable tribe, free of crime,
Our jaunt had turned from a laugh
Into a veritable bloodbath.

With new light we sighted Venice,
Your fever had become a menace,
We moored at our earliest chance
As I called a water-ambulance,
To a private clinic you were raced
And in the care of an agèd doctor placed,
He immediately put you on a drip
And from consciousness you began to slip.

A vigil at your bedside I kept up day and night,
Your condition gave me constant cause for fright,
Although I had done as much as I could
I hadn't cleansed your wounds as well as I should,
Weird words poured from your mouth as you lay in bed,
I mopped your brow, my hand on your head,
It was some days before an improvement could be seen,
Opening your eyes, you said—Cam, where've you been?

Your gradual recovery gave me hope,
Without you I feared I could not cope,
I told you everything would be OK,

That soon again, we'd be on our way,
Our voyage through life would not end
And you would always be my friend,
But from the fog in your eyes I could tell
That you were *very* far from well.

Through the night you ranted and raved,
Bathed in sweat for your demons you slaved,
Your unconscious mind in pain was screaming,
Who knows what tortures you were dreaming?
I lay awake, waiting for your fit to subside,
By you I had sworn to abide,
In the early morning I finally slept
As you awoke and from the clinic crept.

The Doctor shook me awake, saying—Signore B has gone!
There were only crumpled sheets for us to look upon,
I was appalled by what the Doc had said to me,
—How did B get out? I asked furiously,
The Doctor claimed—While Nurse answered nature's call,
—He left through the fire exit in no time at all,
I spotted the note at your bedside,
The words you'd penned left me mortified.

—My Dear Cam, you wrote—I must away,
—I need to catch and butcher The Ram,
—For his heinous crimes he will pay
—Or I'm not the man you think I am,

—How I'll finish him I cannot say,
—If it's long and painful, I don't give a damn,
—Impaled rear to mouth above a gentle blaze,
—Spit-roasted alive for hours and days.

—B's gone insane, I said—We must stop him
—Before he barbecues his foe, body and limb,
—Or The Ram shoots B in the head
—And dumps him in a skip, bloodied and dead,
—To prevent tragedy we haven't much time,
—We must avert a barbaric crime,
—Come on, Doc, don't procrastinate!
—Let's find your patient before it's too late!

I ran to *The Bolivar* and raised the crew,
All over town we searched the streets for you,
The old doctor did not help a jot,
Proving as useful as a chocolate teapot,
Leaving him we bribed the gondoliers
Who acted as Venice's eyes and ears,
Receiving a reported sighting, I ran to see
With a sense someone was following me.

Soon I was lost in a web of alleyways
Seeking an address in that hopeless maze,
Desperate was I to find you
Before more mayhem could ensue,
In my bones I felt you were in danger
When I ran into a familiar *stranger*
Who said—I believe I can be of help,
It was The Wolf! I let out a yelp.

—You, b'stard, I said—Keep away from me,
—To flee you, we sailed across the sea,
Coolly, he replied—If I can ask you to stop,
—It's all right; I'm an undercover cop!
He flashed his badge but I couldn't understand,
Why a policeman would be so underhand,
The Wolf said—My name's Constantino,
—Now I shall tell you all you wish to know.

The detective led me to a café
Promising my doubts to allay,
—For two years, he said—I've tried to infiltrate
—A drugs cartel that's both global and great
—In size, and led by an evil man;
—The fiend you know as The Ram,
—Becoming *The Wolf* let me win the trust
—Of members of his gang we wanted to bust.

—At the Death Slam I acted tough, he said,
—But I wouldn't have shot you or B dead,
—As a teenager I'd won many a poetry slam,
—So it was easy for me to stage that sham,
I asked—What about your *sister* and your *wife*?
—The women who gave us the loving of our life,
He said—I'm sorry to have taken you in,
—They work for me, those ladies of sin.

Constantino said—Call me Con, you may,
I said—After your deceit it seems apt, anyway!
Con said—What surprised me was that you put to sea

—To sail to Kefalonia where The Ram proved to be,
—We suspected you were mixed up with his drugs ring
—But Athina assured me you did not know a thing,
—*Athina?* I gasped, as the penny began to drop,
—Please don't tell me *she's* an undercover cop.

Con said—She's an outstanding officer, devoted to the cause,
—Athina sacrifices herself to uphold our laws,
I choked—That's all very well; the logic I can see
—But are there any of your team who *haven't* bedded me?
—Will I find my 'ex', Lorraine, was an undercover 'tec
—Who dumped me for a new lead, leaving me a wreck?
—Is my entire love life down to your investigation?
—Your probe a panacea for my sexual frustration?

—Calm yourself, said Con—I've never heard of Lorraine,
—It was just the girls I mentioned and shan't happen again,
—Listen! Athina's in grave danger and that's a fact,
—With her backup team she's completely lost contact,
—For two days now we haven't spoken,
—I fear her cover may be broken,
—We must find her and B before it's too late,
—We need to help each other; please don't hesitate!

We rose and got the hell out of there
Feeling better in the Venetian air,
Con had grasped the city's geography,
A skill that put him streets ahead of me,
We found the door where you'd last been seen,
Con kicked it in like it was made of Plasticine,
Inside was a small apartment, rarely used I'd say,
—This ain't all, hollered Con—No bloody way!

Like a Whirling Dervish he pulled up the rugs
And cut up the carpets, disturbing the bugs,
I asked—What makes you so sure Athina was here?
Con said—Her sweet aroma lingers, in the atmos-
    phere,
Now he said it, there was the faintest scent
Of Athina's perfume, lusty and opulent,
With an iron crowbar, Con ripped up the floor
Till I shifted a cabinet to find a trapdoor.

Con pulled the ring and up the lid flipped:
A foot-square portal through which we slipped,
In dread we descended a ladder of steel,
The door slammed above us; testing our zeal,
Deeper and danker in darkness we sank,
—For this madness, I thought—I've a copper to
    thank,
—Cam, said Con—I can feel another hatch,
—I paused above him as he struck a match.

This one was different; it was on the tunnel's side,
—That's good, I said—Let's look inside,

Con pulled it open to reveal a downward slope,
—What do you reckon? he asked—Take it and hope?
I was not sure; it was impossible to tell
Which way held salvation and which a bloody hell,
—You decide, Con, I said—You're the cop,
—I'm feeling claustrophobic and want this to stop.

So I suppose I did decide,
The two of us climbed on the slide,
Sarcastically, I mumbled—This will be fun,
Descending like snowboarders on a black run,
Down and round and round we went,
The slide was like a corkscrew bent,
We skidded off the end at a cracking rate,
Breaking our fall were soft boxes and a crate.

—Ah, the trash has arrived, said The Ram,
Con and I had found our man!
We dusted ourselves down, adjusting to the light,
After the shaft's darkness it was blinding bright,
We were in a utility room some thirty-foot square,
A door was open and The Ram stood there,
The devil grinned and brandished a gun,
—What's kept you? he asked—I've already begun.

With a wave of gun barrel he made us go with him
Into his lair; what horrors lay within?
A catacomb of rooms, whitewashed and fiercely lit,
No furniture or pictures; nowhere to eat or sit,
He led us to a chamber with a blood-red curtain at
    its end,

A noxious smell assailed our nostrils, starkly to offend,
He smiled—I expect you think I should employ a
   cleaner,
—Or are wondering: where is *our* girl Athina?

Now I could see how badly I'd scourged his head,
His scars were plump and purple or septic grey like
   lead,
—What a beast I've turned into, I thought to myself,
—This is what happens when freedom is your wealth!
I guessed Con was longing to ask about our former
   lover
But dared not for fear of blowing her cover,
The Ram said—You've both treated me like a sackless
   fool
—But you'll see soon who's the flaccid tool.

—I have known for months that Athina's a copper
—But let her live to see you come a cropper,
—Do you think that if her betrayal had been in
   doubt
—I would have decided to pimp her out
—To you, Chancer Cam, a British government
   flunky?
—Yes, I know *all* about you, Minister junkie!
—And, you, so-called Wolf, had Athina years before,
—The tragedy is you'll be having her no more.

—Please spare her, begged Con—She saved your life
—And I love her; for years she was my wife!
—Kill me instead! Get it off your chest!

—I'm sure you can see that'd be for the best,
The Ram said—Wolf, your courage does you credit,
—Alas, it's too late; her fate I cannot edit,
Slowly he raised the curtain to reveal,
A sight so shocking it appeared unreal.

Athina was suspended upside down by twin rope;
A bloodied 'Y', beaten way beyond hope,
—My God, I cried out, staggered by her state,
—You're a psycho, eaten up by hate,
Yet, her beautiful face he had left free of mark,
The contrast with her body was shockingly stark,
The Ram laughed—As you can see, Athina cannot survive
—But for you to say goodbye I've kept her just alive.

—ATHINA! shouted Con, preparing to fight,
—IT'S NOT OVER! YOU'LL BE ALL RIGHT!
I swear I saw her half-flicker an eye
As The Ram shot Con, snarling—Die, *Lupus*, die!
Con fell but crawled on, clutching for her hand,
True love, I guess, few can understand,
I lunged at The Ram who pistol-whipped me as I got near,
And with a barber's razor, cut *her* throat from ear to ear.

I tried in vain to get to her
But my sight was just a blur,
Blood gushed down her lovely head,
Soon I knew she would be dead,

I said—For God's sake, what have you done?
The Ram sneered—Cam, I've almost won,
I believe I passed out, totally out of breath
As Athina drew her last, and bravely met her death.

I came round to find myself in a cell,
Struggling to remember and feeling unwell,
As recent events drifted back to me
The full horror replayed too readily,
I felt depressed that moment like at no other,
I needed you near, B, my soul brother,
I prayed you would come to my aid
Before my will to live did finally fade.

Now I know what's done we cannot undo,
The time for heroism is through,
My spell on this planet has almost passed,
All I do now is write and fast,
The Ram is keeping me alive to draw you in,
He said—What I'll do to that man I can't begin
—To tell you; B's dangerous and bad,
I said—No, Ram, you're the one who's mad!

The Ram gave me pen, paper and ink,
He ordered—Write B a letter to make him think,
This I do, and beg you *not* to come,
Save yourself this time, my dear chum!
I have not eaten for ten days,
Soon, B, we'll go different ways,
But I want you to know I could never regret
That glorious day on the train when we met.

It seems an aeon ago that I rode The Six Fifty-Three
Where finding a seat gave secretive glee
And the presence of a pretty girl
Threw my feelings int' a whirl,
You whisked me off onto your ship,
Taught me to DJ and how to be hip,
I was so much happier than I'd been before
As a craven, pen-pushing Civil Service bore.

Routine is again the main man,
Food arrives; I throw it at The Ram,
I refuse to live as his pawn
Or to die, throat gaping and torn,
What fun we enjoyed back in Lisbon,
Even if we were by cops put upon,
And in Kefalonia by a beauty I was seduced
Little knowing, less caring I was being traduced.

I am getting weak, B; I can barely write,
The end is nigh, I've quit the fight,
The Ram has a *special treat* waiting for you,
He'll skin you alive if you come to my rescue;
Now I am delusional, day-dreaming of Elvis again,
What would the Minister have made of a goat on
    cocaine?
Or our battle with pirates on the high seas?
Those brigands we slew in their twos and their
    threes.

On my deathbed you shine as a vision from my past,
My constitution's shot, no longer shall I last,

Now I have so little left to do and say,
With every pen stroke, my strength ebbs away,
So farewell, Dear-heart, I pray this letter survives,
Our short time together was worth a thousand boring lives,
With you, Byron, I lived like a lion, not an office mouse,

    Yours, *Amico Amante In Eterno,*

John Cam Hobhouse

British poet **Oliver Gozzard** has enjoyed a nomadic existence, living in Oxford, Poole, Hull, Cardiff, Coventry, London, Lutterworth, Leamington Spa, and now Lewes. His heroes are Lord Byron and Philip Larkin, who once described him as a 'very rude young man'. *The Commuter's Tale* is Gozzard's first book and was written on the train.